SO YOU WANT TO BE A COACH...

(An introduction to coaching)

Phil Cusack

CONTENTS

SO YOU WANT TO BE A COACH…

(An introduction to coaching)

Phil Cusack

DISCOVERING THE UNIVERSE OF COACHING

Welcome to a fascinating journey into the vast and enriching world of coaching. In the pages that follow, we will dive into the deep waters of a transformative practice that has changed the lives of countless people around the world. What is coaching and why have so many found it a beacon of guidance in their lives?

The Art of Coaching:

At its core, coaching is an art. It is the art of personal transformation, the mastery of self-reflection and the science of unlocking human potential. Through intentional collaboration between coach and client, space is opened to explore, question and grow. Coaching goes beyond finding answers; It is a journey towards clarity, discovery and action.

The Fundamental Purpose:

The fundamental purpose of coaching is simple but powerful: to guide people toward a fuller, more meaningful life. It is a tool that drives positive change, encourages personal and professional development, and provides support at crucial moments in life. Instead of imposing answers, coaching illuminates the path for each individual to discover their own solutions and potential.

The Journey of Twenty Disciplines:

As we dive into this book, we will embark on a journey through twenty unique coaching disciplines. Each discipline is like a bright constellation in the coaching sky, offering different lights and guidance. From Life Coaching, which charts a course toward meaningful goals, to Transformation Coaching, which invites profound evolution, each discipline focuses on specific areas of our lives.

The Promise of Exploration:

This book is an invitation to exploration. Through its pages, you will discover how coaching can impact areas as diverse as interpersonal communication, parenting, health and well-being, and more. Each discipline has its own story to tell, its own lessons to offer and its own paths to explore.

A Future of Possibilities:

As you dive into these disciplines, consider this more than a book; It is a map that will guide you through the vast territory of coaching. Imagine a future where your goals become tangible, where challenges become opportunities, and where your life takes the shape you've always wanted. This is the potential of coaching.

Your Journey Starts Here:

Get ready to embark on a journey of self-discovery, growth, and unlimited possibilities. Each page you read will bring you closer to a deeper understanding of yourself and the powerful tools that coaching has to offer. The promise is simple but profound: coaching can be the catalyst that transforms your life.

So go forth, intrepid explorer! Let this book be the first page of your own story of transformation through coaching. With each discipline, you will find new layers of meaning and new opportunities to evolve. Welcome to the universe of coaching, where the possibilities are endless and your journey is about to begin!

WHAT IS COACHING?

Coaching is a personal and professional development process that seeks to enhance a person's performance, growth and well-being. Through conversation sessions, a coach works with the client to help them identify and achieve specific goals, overcome obstacles and improve their performance in various areas of life, such as work, personal, academic, among others. .

Coaching focuses on the present and the future, rather than the past, and is based on the premise that each individual has the resources and responses necessary to achieve their goals. The coach facilitates the process of reflection and self-exploration, asking powerful questions that guide the client toward awareness, goal clarification, and identification of concrete actions.

There are different approaches and specializations within coaching, which can address specific areas such as executive coaching, life coaching, business coaching, sports coaching, among others. Each type of coaching is tailored to clients' particular needs and focuses on specific aspects of their lives.

It is important to note that coaching is not therapy or advice. While therapy may focus on resolving emotional or psychological issues from the past, and counseling provides guidance and advice, coaching focuses on developing skills, setting goals, and maximizing the individual's potential in the present and future. .

In addition to the distinction between coaching, therapy, and counseling, it is essential to understand the collaborative relationship between the coach and the client. In this process, the coach acts as an objective facilitator who provides support, motivation and structure, but the client is the one who leads the way and makes informed decisions to achieve their goals.

Coaching can be done individually or in groups, and sessions are usually confidential. As the process progresses, the client may experience significant changes in their perspective, behaviors, and outcomes, contributing to greater self-awareness and empowerment.

Key skills of a coach include active listening, empathy, asking powerful questions, the ability to set clear goals, and facilitating positive change. These professionals adhere to a code of ethics that respects client confidentiality and integrity.

WHAT QUALITIES SHOULD A GOOD COACH HAVE?

A good coach must possess a variety of skills and qualities to be effective in their role as a facilitator of their clients' personal and professional development. Some of the essential qualities of a good coach include:

1. Empathy: The ability to understand and empathize with the customer's experience and perspectives is crucial. The coach must be able to connect emotionally with the client to provide genuine support.

2. Active listening: A good coach listens attentively and thoughtfully. Active listening involves paying full attention to what the client is communicating, both verbally and non-verbally, to fully understand their situation and needs.

3. Clarity of communication: The coach must be able to communicate clearly and effectively. This involves the ability to convey information in an understandable way and to use language that resonates with the customer.

4. Questioning Skills: Asking powerful, thoughtful questions is essential to helping the client explore their thoughts, feelings, and goals. Open-ended, challenging questions can lead to greater awareness and clarity.

5. Goal orientation: A good coach works with the client to establish clear and achievable goals. You must guide the client in creating an effective action plan and motivate them to follow it.

6. Integrity and ethics: Honesty and integrity are fundamental in the coach-client relationship. A good coach must maintain confidentiality, be transparent and act ethically at all times.

7. Flexibility and adaptability: Each client is unique, and a good coach should be able to adapt their approach according to the individual needs of each person. Flexibility allows you to adjust the coaching process to achieve the best results.

8. Inspiration and motivation: A good coach must be able to inspire and motivate the client. This involves fostering a positive environment, recognizing achievements and helping the client overcome challenges.

9. Technical knowledge and skills: The coach must possess a solid knowledge of coaching techniques, as well as specific skills related to the client's profession or area of focus.

10. Self-awareness: An effective coach must be aware of their own beliefs, values and biases, as this can influence their interaction with the client. Self-awareness allows the coach to manage their own emotions and maintain focus on the client's needs.

These combined qualities contribute to the creation of a strong and effective coaching relationship, where the client feels supported and empowered to achieve their goals.

WHAT OBJECTIVES SHOULD A GOOD COACH HAVE?

A good coach should have a series of clear objectives aimed at maximizing the potential of their clients. These objectives include:

1. Facilitate Self-Knowledge: Help the client understand their strengths, weaknesses, values, beliefs and motivations. Self-knowledge is essential to make informed decisions and set goals aligned with personal values.

2. Establish Clear Goals: Collaborate with the client to define specific, measurable, achievable, relevant goals with defined deadlines (SMART methodology). These goals provide clear and measurable direction for the coaching process.

3. Promote Awareness: Help the client explore their thoughts, emotions and behaviors. Awareness facilitates change by identifying patterns and beliefs that may be limiting progress.

4. Develop Skills: Work on the development of specific skills that allow the client to achieve their goals. This may include leadership skills, communication, problem solving, time management, among others.

5. Promote Autonomy: Empower the client to make informed decisions and take responsibility for their own development. The goal is for the client to become more independent and self-sufficient in achieving their goals.

6. Provide Constructive Feedback: Provide honest and constructive feedback to support client growth and learning. This includes recognizing achievements, identifying areas for improvement, and celebrating progress.

7. Promote Positive Change: Help the client overcome obstacles, adopt new perspectives and make positive changes in their life. Coaching seeks to promote personal and professional growth in a sustainable way.

8. Improve Self-Confidence: Work on strengthening the client's self-confidence and self-esteem. Increasing self-confidence can be a key factor in overcoming challenges and taking on new challenges.

9. Support Stress Management: Provide tools and strategies to manage stress and pressure effectively. This may include time management techniques, mindfulness, or other practices that contribute to balance and well-being.

10. Promote Sustainability: Collaborate in creating changes that are sustainable in the long term. Coaching not only focuses on short-term solutions, but on developing lasting habits and behaviors.

These goals are designed to improve the client's quality of life, effectiveness, and overall well-being. A good coach adapts these objectives to the specific needs and aspirations of each individual who seeks guidance.

WHAT SHOULD A GOOD COACH AVOID?

A good coach must avoid certain behaviors and practices to maintain the integrity of the coaching relationship and ensure a supportive and growing environment for the client. Here are some things a good coach should avoid:

1. Imposing Solutions: Avoid providing direct answers or imposing solutions on the client. The objective is to guide the client to discover their own responses and strategies, promoting autonomy.

2. Lack of Active Listening: Avoid constant interruptions or lack of attention during sessions. Active listening is essential to fully understand the client's perspective and offer meaningful guidance.

3. Judgments and Prejudices: Avoid judging the client or expressing prejudices. A good coach maintains an objective and non-judgmental approach to create an environment of trust and openness.

4. Lack of Empathy: Avoid a lack of empathy towards the client's experiences and challenges. Empathy is crucial to building a strong connection and showing genuine understanding.

5. Breach of Confidentiality: Do not share confidential client information without their consent. Confidentiality is essential to establish a safe and trusting environment.

6. Lack of Clarity in Roles and Limits: Avoid a lack of clarity about the roles and limits of coaching. It is essential to set clear expectations about what the client can expect from the coach and vice versa.

7. Giving Unsolicited Advice: Avoid giving unsolicited advice or becoming an expert in the client's specific area. Coaching focuses on the process and not on providing direct solutions.

8. Lack of Adaptability: Not being inflexible in approach. A good coach should adapt to the client's individual needs rather than following a rigid approach.

9. Lack of Self-Awareness: Avoid a lack of self-awareness about one's own beliefs and values. A coach must recognize and manage his or her own biases so as not to negatively influence the coaching process.

10. Lack of Technical Skill: Not possessing the necessary skills and knowledge. A good coach must be well trained and up-to-date in coaching techniques and practices.

11. Impatience: Avoid impatience or pressuring the client to achieve quick results. The coaching process requires time and patience to achieve significant and sustainable changes.

By avoiding these behaviors, a coach can contribute to a positive, respectful, and growth-focused coaching environment.

WHAT SHOULD WE STUDY TO BE A GOOD COACH?

To become a good coach, it is advisable to acquire a combination of theoretical knowledge and practical skills. Here are some key areas of study and development:

1. Coaching Training: Look for recognized and accredited coaching training programs. Many institutions offer coaching certifications that cover both theory and practical skills.

2. Psychology and Human Behavior: Studying psychology provides a deep understanding of the human mind, motivations and behavioral patterns. This is essential to understanding customer needs and perspectives.

3. Effective Communication: Developing effective communication skills is crucial to being a good coach. Studying interpersonal communication, active listening, empathy, and questioning techniques can significantly improve these skills.

4. Theories of Learning and Development: Understanding the theories of human learning and development provides a solid foundation to guide clients in their personal and professional growth.

5. Ethics in Coaching: Studying and understanding the ethical principles of coaching is essential. Ethics in coaching include confidentiality, respect and integrity.

6. Non-Verbal Communication Skills: Learning to interpret and use non-verbal communication can improve a coach's ability to understand clients' emotions and needs.

7. Time Management and Planning: Developing time management and planning skills is important to help clients set goals and create effective action plans.

8. Leadership and Personal Development: Studying theories of leadership and personal development can provide valuable tools for working with clients seeking to improve in these areas.

9. Specialized Coaching: Depending on your interests and professional goals, consider the possibility of specializing in specific areas of coaching, such as executive coaching, life coaching, business coaching, sports coaching, among others.

10. Practical Practice and Supervision: Practical experience is essential. Look for opportunities to conduct coaching sessions, whether through supervised internships,

mentoring, or working with real clients.

11. Continuous Development: The field of coaching is constantly evolving. Participate in continuous development programs, attend conferences, seminars and workshops to stay up to date on the latest trends and best practices in coaching.

The combination of theory and practice, along with an ongoing commitment to professional development, can help you build the skills and knowledge necessary to become a good coach. It is also important to obtain recognized certifications in coaching to support your credibility in the field.

WHAT WOULD BE INTERESTING TO STUDY TO BE A GOOD COACH?

In addition to the specific areas related to coaching, there are additional disciplines and skills that can enrich a coach's practice and improve their effectiveness. Here are some suggestions:

1. Neuroscience: Understanding the fundamentals of neuroscience can provide insights into how the brain works and how people learn and change. This can improve your ability to personalize coaching approaches.

2. Emotional Intelligence: Studying emotional intelligence will allow you to understand and help clients manage their emotions, as well as develop key emotional skills such as empathy and self-regulation.

3. Mindfulness and Positive Psychology: Integrating mindfulness practices and positive psychology principles

can contribute to the client's overall well-being and offer practical tools for personal development.

4. Resilience: Studying resilience can help you guide clients through challenges and foster resilience in difficult situations.

5. Nonviolent Communication (NVC): NVC provides a framework for effective and respectful communication. It can be a valuable tool to improve communication with customers.

6. Systems Theory and Group Dynamics: Understanding how systems and groups work can be beneficial, especially if you work with teams or in organizational settings.

7. Relaxation and Stress Management Techniques: Knowing practical relaxation and stress management techniques can be useful in supporting clients in challenging situations.

8. Team Coaching: If you are interested in team coaching, studying group dynamics, team development, and team leadership can be beneficial.

9. Negotiation and Conflict Resolution: Acquiring skills in negotiation and conflict resolution can be useful, especially if you work with clients in work or interpersonal relationships settings.

10. Organizational Change: Understanding the principles

of organizational change can be valuable if you specialize in organizational or executive coaching.

11. Organizational Culture: Studying organizational culture can help you adapt your coaching approach to align with the specific characteristics and values of an organization.

12. Information Technologies and Virtual Platforms: Given the growing popularity of online coaching, familiarizing yourself with information technologies and virtual platforms can be useful.

Remember that coaching is an interdisciplinary field, and the diversity of knowledge can broaden your skills and approaches. Combining coaching competencies with a broader understanding of related disciplines can enhance your ability to address the diverse needs of your clients.

WHY ARE COACHES SO CRITICIZED BY PSYCHOLOGISTS?

Criticism of coaches by some psychologists may have various reasons, and it is important to note that opinions can vary widely in both camps. Some of the reasons that have been mentioned for the criticism include:

1. Lack of Regulation: Unlike psychology, which generally has a stricter regulatory framework and licensing requirements, the coaching profession is less regulated. This has led to concerns about the lack of uniform standards and training requirements in the coaching industry.

2. Differences in Training: Some psychologists criticize the variability in the quality and depth of coaching training. While some coaches have completed robust, accredited training programs, others may not have the same academic and theoretical background as psychologists.

3. Differential Approach: Clinical and therapeutic psychology tends to have a more in-depth and

treatment-oriented approach to mental health problems, while coaching often focuses on personal development, performance and goal achievement. Some psychologists may consider that coaching does not adequately address deeper psychological issues.

4. Role Confusion: There is concern that some coaches, especially those who are not sufficiently trained, may cross boundaries and address topics that are outside their scope. This could result in a lack of adequate attention to mental health problems that require therapeutic intervention.

5. Use of Non-Scientific Techniques: Some psychologists criticize the inclusion of non-scientific techniques or techniques without empirical support in the field of coaching. While psychology tends to rely on methods backed by scientific research, some coaches may use approaches that lack empirical evidence.

Importantly, there are many psychologists and coaching professionals who recognize and respect the differences between the two disciplines and can collaborate effectively. Additionally, some coaches have training in psychology or related fields, and some psychologists have incorporated elements of coaching into their practice.

The key to an effective relationship between both fields lies in mutual respect, understanding the differences in approaches and collaboration when appropriate, recognizing the ethical and professional limits of each profession.

Despite criticism, we must not forget that the coaching profession, like psychology, plays a valuable role in supporting people's personal and professional development. Although I recognize the concerns expressed by some psychologists, I believe it is essential to highlight the positive and beneficial aspects of coaching as a complementary discipline. Here are some points that might help defend the coaching profession:

1. Focus on Development and Empowerment: Coaching focuses on personal growth, goal setting and empowerment. Unlike psychology, which often addresses mental health issues, coaching is geared toward continuous improvement, optimizing performance, and achieving specific goals.

2. Future Orientation: While psychology can look to the past to understand and treat problems, coaching focuses on the present and the future. We help clients identify clear goals and take action to achieve positive results in their lives.

3. Collaboration and Partner in Change: Coaching is based on a collaborative relationship between the coach and the client. I act as a partner in change, guiding the client through reflective processes, exploration of options and informed decision making.

4. Promoting Self-Awareness and Responsibility: Coaching seeks to raise the client's self-awareness and encourage the assumption of responsibility for their actions and choices.

We help clients better understand themselves and take proactive steps to achieve their goals.

5. Flexibility and Adaptability: Coaching is flexible and adapts to the individual needs of each client. Through a variety of approaches and techniques, coaches can customize their strategies to meet each person's unique needs.

6. Holistic Approach: Many coaches take a holistic approach, taking into account the entirety of an individual's life, including their professional goals, personal relationships, well-being and personal development. This comprehensive approach can have a positive impact on various areas of life.

7. Fostering Latent Potential: Coaching recognizes and fosters the latent potential in each individual. We work to unlock internal skills, talents and resources that may be underutilized or overlooked.

8. Developing Practical Skills and Strategies: Coaches often provide practical skills and strategies that clients can apply in their everyday lives. This practical approach can lead to tangible and sustainable results.

In this way, coaching offers a complementary approach to psychology, focusing on development, empowerment and continuous improvement. Both disciplines, when practiced ethically, can coexist harmoniously and contribute to the comprehensive well-being of people.

WHAT ARE THE MAIN DISCIPLINES OF COACHING?

Coaching is a broad and diverse discipline that encompasses various specializations to suit the specific needs of clients. Here are some of the main disciplines of coaching, each with a brief description:

1. Life Coaching: Focuses on personal development and general well-being. Life coaches work with clients to set personal goals, improve self-esteem, balance life, and achieve a greater sense of fulfillment.

2. Executive Coaching: Aimed at professionals and leaders in the business field. Executive coaches work on developing leadership skills, time management, decision making, and other competencies relevant to success in corporate environments.

3. Business Coaching: Aimed at business owners, entrepreneurs and professionals in the business world. Business coaches help improve business performance, strategic planning, decision making and leadership in the

business environment.

4. Sports Coaching: Focused on athletes and sports teams. Sports coaches work on skill development, motivation, performance management and overcoming mental obstacles to improve sports performance.

5. Educational Coaching: Aimed at students, educators and professionals in the educational field. Educational coaches support academic development, educational decision making, and balance between academic and personal life.

6. Career Coaching: Focuses on professional development and career management. Career coaches help individuals explore career options, set career goals, and overcome obstacles in their career path.

7. Health and Wellness Coaching: Oriented towards improving health and well-being. Health coaches work with clients to establish health goals, lifestyle changes, stress management, and improving overall well-being.

8. Relationship Coaching: Focused on improving personal relationships and communication. Relationship coaches work with individuals or couples to strengthen bonds, overcome challenges, and improve the quality of relationships.

9. Personal Finance Coaching: Focuses on financial management and setting financial goals. Personal finance coaches help clients develop financial skills, set budgets, and achieve financial goals.

10. Diversity and Inclusion Coaching: Aimed at organizations and professionals interested in promoting diversity and inclusion. Coaches in this field work on creating inclusive work cultures and managing diversity in the work environment.

11. Emotional Intelligence Coaching: It focuses on the development of emotional intelligence, including emotional awareness, emotional management and the relationship with one's own and others' emotions.

12. Coaching in Sustainable Development: Aimed at individuals and organizations committed to sustainable practices. Sustainable development coaches work on the integration of sustainable practices and social responsibility.

13. Entrepreneurship Coaching: Aimed at entrepreneurs and startups. Entrepreneurship coaches help develop business skills, overcome challenges, and establish strategies for business success.

14. Creativity Coaching: Focuses on unleashing creativity and innovation. Creativity coaches work with individuals and teams to enhance creativity and find innovative solutions.

15. Change Management Coaching: Aimed at individuals and organizations facing significant changes. Change management coaches help manage transitions, overcome resistance and adapt to new environments.

16. Conflict Resolution Coaching: Focused on addressing and resolving interpersonal conflicts. Conflict resolution coaches work on developing communication skills and constructively managing disputes.

17. Transformation Coaching: Focuses on facilitating deep changes and personal transformations. Transformation coaches work on deeper aspects of personal and spiritual development.

18. Mindfulness Coaching: Aimed at integrating mindfulness practices into daily life. Mindfulness coaches help cultivate mindfulness to reduce stress and improve well-being.

19. Coaching in Interpersonal Communication: Aimed at improving communication skills in the personal and professional sphere. Interpersonal communication coaches work on developing active listening, empathy, and communicative clarity.

20. Parenting Coaching: Focuses on supporting parents and families. Parenting coaches work on developing parenting skills, managing family stress, and improving family dynamics.

These disciplines reflect the diversity and breadth of applications of coaching in various aspects of life and work. We are going to detail each one of them.

LIFE COACHING

Life Coaching is a coaching discipline that focuses on personal development, improving the quality of life and achieving individual goals. Unlike therapy, which often focuses on resolving emotional or psychological problems, life coaching is future-oriented, seeking to enhance a person's strengths and abilities to reach their full potential.

What is it for:

Life Coaching serves to help people identify and achieve their personal and professional goals, improve decision making, increase self-awareness, and develop greater balance and well-being in various areas of their lives. It is based on the principle that each individual has the ability to create the life they want and to overcome obstacles that may arise along the way.

Goals:

- Establish clear and achievable goals.

- Improve self-confidence and self-esteem.

- Develop effective decision-making skills.

- Create and maintain healthy personal relationships.

- Balance personal and professional life.

- Overcome obstacles and limitations.

- Promote personal growth and development.

Who is it intended for:

Life Coaching is intended for anyone seeking to improve specific aspects of their life, address personal challenges, or simply achieve a higher level of satisfaction and fulfillment in their daily life. There are no restrictions regarding age, profession or personal situation; It is accessible to any individual who is willing to commit to their own development.

How can you help:

- Clarify personal goals and values.

- Overcome procrastination and establish effective routines.

- Improve interpersonal communication skills.

- Develop strategies to manage stress and anxiety.

- Address balance challenges between personal and professional life.

- Promote positive changes in habits and lifestyle.

- Establish healthy boundaries in personal relationships.

- Explore and enhance talents and skills.

How does this work:

- Individual Sessions: Life coaching sessions are normally individual and personalized, focused on the client's specific needs.

- Interviews and Reflective Questioning: The coach uses powerful questions to help the client reflect on their current situation, identify goals and explore possible solutions.

- Establishment of SMART Goals: We work on defining specific, measurable, achievable, relevant and time-bound goals (SMART), providing a clear structure for progress.

- Action Plan and Responsibility: A detailed action plan is created that the client follows between sessions. The coach provides support and responsibility to ensure the implementation of concrete actions.

- Constructive Feedback: Constructive feedback and ongoing support is provided to celebrate achievements, adjust approaches and overcome challenges.

- Practical Tools and Exercises: The coach can use various practical tools and exercises to strengthen skills, improve self-awareness and facilitate positive change.

Life Coaching is a powerful tool for those seeking personalized support to move toward their goals and create a more fulfilling and meaningful life.

EXECUTIVE COACHING

Executive Coaching is a coaching discipline designed specifically for professionals in leadership roles, executives, and individuals seeking to maximize their performance in organizational settings. This type of coaching focuses on developing leadership skills, effective management, and improving executive performance to achieve organizational and personal goals.

What is it for:

Executive Coaching serves to enhance leadership skills, improve strategic decision making, increase effectiveness in team management, and address specific challenges that leaders face in their professional roles.

Goals:

- Develop and improve leadership skills.

- Increase emotional and social intelligence.

- Improve strategic decision making.

- Facilitate adaptability and change management.

- Promote effectiveness in executive communication.

- Optimize time management and productivity.

- Facilitate the development of key executive competencies.

Who is it intended for:

Executive Coaching is intended for leaders, executives and senior professionals seeking personalized support to achieve specific goals in their roles and contribute to organizational success. It can be beneficial for leaders at any level, from senior executives to middle managers.

How can you help:

- Develop an effective and authentic leadership style.

- Improve communication with teams and colleagues.

- Address specific challenges in team management.

- Facilitate transition to higher leadership roles.

- Improve delegation and empowerment skills.

- Develop strategies for the management of organizational change.

- Increase resilience and adaptability in dynamic environments.

How does this work:

- Personalized Sessions: Executive Coaching sessions are personalized and adapted to the specific goals and challenges of the executive.

- Competency Evaluation: An initial evaluation of the competencies and areas for improvement is carried out, identifying clear objectives for coaching.

- 360 Degree Feedback: 360 degree feedback can be incorporated to obtain perspectives from colleagues, subordinates and superiors, providing a complete view of the executive's performance.

- Executive Action Plan Development: Work is being done to create a strategic action plan that addresses specific areas of improvement and capitalizes on the executive's strengths.

- Continuous Monitoring and Evaluation: The coach performs regular follow-ups, adjusts the action plan as necessary and provides continuous feedback to ensure the effectiveness of the coaching process.

- Integration into the Organizational Context: Executive Coaching is often integrated into the organizational context, aligning individual objectives with the company's objectives.

Executive Coaching is a powerful tool for leaders seeking to optimize their performance, develop strategic skills, and address specific challenges in their leadership roles.

BUSINESS COACHING

Business Coaching is a specialized branch of coaching that focuses on improving business performance, organizational effectiveness and the overall success of companies. This type of coaching works with business leaders, entrepreneurs, and teams to address specific challenges, develop effective strategies, and maximize growth potential.

What is it for:

Business Coaching serves to enhance business leadership, optimize strategic decision making, improve operational efficiency, and overcome specific obstacles that can affect the performance and growth of the company.

Goals:

- Develop strategies for business growth.

- Improve decision making and financial management.

- Optimize operational efficiency and productivity.

- Promote effective leadership in business environments.

- Address specific market and competitive challenges.

- Facilitate the transition to new stages of business development.

Who is it intended for:

Business Coaching is intended for business owners, entrepreneurs, business leaders and teams seeking to improve the performance and effectiveness of their organizations. It is relevant to companies of all sizes and at various stages of development.

How can you help:

- Develop strategic plans for business growth.

- Improve team management and organizational dynamics.

- Optimize internal processes to increase efficiency.

- Facilitate financial planning and resource management.

- Address challenges in entering new markets.

- Develop strategies for the management of organizational change.

- Overcome specific obstacles in business development.

How does this work:

- Business Analysis and Diagnosis: An exhaustive analysis of the company is carried out, identifying areas for improvement and opportunities for growth.

- Definition of Business Goals: Clear goals and objectives are established, aligned with the vision and mission of the company, to guide the coaching process.

- Development of Business Strategies: We work on creating specific strategies to address identified challenges and take advantage of growth opportunities.

- Business Leadership Coaching: Focuses on developing leadership skills for business owners and key leaders.

- Implementation of Action Plans: Detailed action plans are developed for the implementation of strategies, with continuous monitoring and adjustment.

- Continuous Evaluation and Improvement: The coaching process includes regular evaluations to measure progress and make adjustments as necessary to achieve business objectives.

Business Coaching is a valuable tool for companies looking to improve their performance, address specific challenges and achieve new levels of success in a competitive business environment.

COACHING DEPORTIVO

Sports Coaching is a specialized discipline of coaching that focuses on supporting athletes, teams and coaches to maximize their sports performance, achieve specific goals and develop mental and emotional skills that contribute to success in the field of sports.

What is it for:

Sports Coaching serves to optimize athletic performance, strengthen mental skills such as concentration and resilience, improve emotional management during competition and provide comprehensive support for the development and success of athletes and teams.

Goals:

- Develop mental and emotional skills.

- Maximize physical and technical performance.

- Improve decision making during the competition.

- Facilitate stress management and competitive pressure.

- Promote teamwork and group cohesion.

- Boost the motivation and confidence of the athlete.

Who is it intended for:

Sports Coaching is intended for athletes of all levels, from amateurs to professionals, as well as coaches and sports teams. It can address a variety of sports, from individual to team, and adapt to the specific needs of each discipline.

How can you help:

- Improve concentration and focus during competition.

- Overcome mental blocks and improve confidence.

- Develop strategies for pre-competition stress management.

- Facilitate emotional recovery after defeats or injuries.

- Strengthen team cohesion and communication skills.

- Establish specific goals for long-term athletic development.

How does this work:

- Performance Evaluation and Objectives: An initial evaluation of sports performance is carried out and clear objectives are established in collaboration with the athlete or team.

- Mental and Emotional Training: Specific mental training techniques are worked on, such as visualization, mindfulness and emotional control, to improve performance and resilience.

- Development of Competition Strategies: Specific

competition situations are addressed and strategies are developed to manage pressure and make effective decisions under stressful conditions.

- Individual and Team Coaching: May include individual sessions with athletes, as well as group sessions to strengthen team cohesion and improve communication.

- Continuous Monitoring and Adjustment: The sports coaching process involves continuous monitoring, adjusting strategies as necessary and constant support for long-term development.

Sports Coaching is an essential tool for athletes and teams looking for a comprehensive approach to improve their performance, manage emotional challenges and achieve their goals in the world of sports.

EDUCATIONAL COACHING

Educational Coaching is a coaching discipline that focuses on supporting students, educators and professionals in the educational field to improve learning, academic performance and personal and professional development.

What is it for:

Educational Coaching serves to improve academic performance, develop effective learning skills, facilitate educational decision making and provide comprehensive support for academic and personal development.

Goals:

- Improve academic performance and understanding of the material.

- Develop study skills and learning techniques.

- Facilitate educational and professional decision-making.

- Promote motivation and commitment to learning.

- Improve communication and teamwork skills in educational environments.

- Address specific challenges in the learning process.

Who is it intended for:

Educational Coaching is intended for students at all levels, from primary school to higher education, as well as educators, teachers, parents and professionals working in the educational field.

How can you help:

- Develop study and time management strategies.

- Overcome mental blocks and fears related to learning.

- Facilitate the transition between educational stages.

- Improve communication and relationship skills in the educational environment.

- Guide in decision-making about careers and specializations.

- Establish short and long-term educational and professional goals.

How does this work:

- Educational Needs Assessment: An initial evaluation of the educational needs and goals of the student or the educational environment in general is carried out.

- Development of Learning Strategies: Personalized strategies are worked on to improve the learning process, including study techniques, organization and time management.

- Individual and Group Coaching: May include individual

sessions with students, teachers or parents, as well as group sessions to improve classroom dynamics or teamwork.

- Support in Educational Decision Making: Guidance and support is provided in making decisions about academic choices, careers, and long-term educational plans.

- Development of Socio-Emotional Skills: Socio-emotional aspects are addressed, such as stress management, self-confidence and social skills, which are fundamental for educational success.

- Continuous Monitoring and Evaluation: The Educational Coaching process includes continuous monitoring to evaluate progress, make adjustments as necessary and provide ongoing support.

Educational Coaching is a valuable tool for students, educators and professionals in the educational field who seek to improve the learning process, overcome challenges and achieve educational and professional goals.

CAREER COACHING

Career Coaching is a coaching discipline that focuses on supporting individuals in the development of their professional career, making decisions related to their career path and maximizing their potential in the professional field.

What is it for:

Career Coaching serves to guide individuals in the design and management of their professional careers, facilitating the exploration of opportunities, informed decision making, and the development of skills necessary for career success.

Goals:

- Identify clear professional goals and objectives.

- Develop strategies for professional advancement and growth.

- Improve career-related decision making.

- Address challenges and obstacles in the professional path.

- Enhance leadership and professional management skills.

- Facilitate the transition between roles or industries.

Who is it intended for:

Career Coaching is intended for professionals at any stage of their career who seek guidance and support in developing, managing and maximizing their career path.

How can you help:

- Identify professional direction and define long-term goals.

- Prepare for job transitions, such as career changes or promotions.

- Develop leadership and management skills to advance your career.

- Improve communication and personal brand in the professional environment.

- Address specific challenges in the workplace or in team management.

- Explore professional and educational development opportunities.

How does this work:

- Evaluation of Skills and Professional Goals: An initial evaluation of the individual's skills, experiences and professional goals is carried out.

- Exploration of Options and Opportunities: We work on exploring career options, identifying opportunities that align with professional objectives.

- Development of a Career Plan: A strategic plan is created for career development, establishing short and long-term goals and the actions necessary to achieve them.

- Development of Skills and Competencies: Key skills necessary for professional success are worked on, such as communication skills, leadership, time management and decision making.

- Interview Preparation and Resume Evaluation: Support is provided in interview preparation, resume review, and developing a solid professional presence.

- Management of Work Transitions: In cases of work transitions, the coach helps manage change, adapt to new circumstances and maximize success in the new position.

- Ongoing Monitoring and Adjustments: The Career Coaching process includes continuous monitoring to evaluate progress, make adjustments as necessary, and provide ongoing support.

Career Coaching is a valuable tool for professionals seeking strategic guidance and personalized support in the management and development of their careers.

HEALTH AND WELLNESS COACHING

Health and Wellbeing Coaching is a specialized branch of coaching that focuses on supporting individuals in improving their physical, mental and emotional health, as well as achieving a general balance that contributes to comprehensive well-being.

What is it for:

Health and Wellness Coaching serves to promote healthy lifestyle habits, manage stress, improve sleep quality, encourage physical activity and facilitate the adoption of behaviors that contribute to general well-being.

Goals:

- Improve physical and mental health.

- Develop healthy and sustainable lifestyle habits.

- Manage stress and promote emotional health.

- Promote physical activity and balanced nutrition.

- Improve sleep quality and time management.

- Address specific challenges related to health and well-being.

Who is it intended for:

Health and Wellness Coaching is intended for anyone seeking to improve their quality of life, adopt healthier habits, and address specific aspects related to physical and mental health.

How can you help:

- Set personalized wellness goals.

- Implement changes in diet and eating habits.

- Develop an exercise plan adapted to individual needs.

- Improve stress management and emotional health.

- Adopt mindfulness and relaxation practices.

- Address specific health challenges, such as weight loss or blood sugar control.

How does this work:

- Comprehensive Health Assessment: An initial assessment of the individual's physical, mental and emotional health is performed, identifying areas for improvement and establishing realistic goals.

- Wellness Goal Development: In collaboration with the client, personalized wellness goals are established that address specific aspects of health and well-being.

- Health and Wellness Plan Design: A detailed action

plan is created that includes dietary changes, exercise plan, stress management strategies and other personalized interventions.

- Support in the Implementation of Changes: The coach provides continuous support to implement the proposed changes, providing guidance, motivation and necessary resources.

- Stress Management Strategies: Stress management techniques, such as mindfulness and relaxation, are worked on to improve emotional and mental health.

- Continuous Monitoring and Evaluation: The Health and Wellness Coaching process includes continuous monitoring to evaluate progress, adjust the plan as necessary and provide ongoing support.

Health and Wellness Coaching is a valuable tool for those looking to improve their health and take a holistic approach to physical and mental well-being.

RELATIONSHIP COACHING

Relationship Coaching is a coaching specialty that focuses on supporting individuals and couples to improve the quality of their personal relationships, whether as a couple, family, friendship or work.

What is it for:

Relationship Coaching serves to strengthen communication, address conflicts, improve emotional connection, and develop skills that contribute to healthier and more satisfying relationships.

Goals:

- Improve communication and active listening.

- Address conflicts and challenges in relationships.

- Develop empathy and understanding skills.

- Strengthen the emotional connection in relationships.

- Improve conflict management and decision making as a couple.

- Foster more positive and satisfying relationships.

Who is it intended for:

Relationship Coaching is intended for individuals, couples, families or teams seeking to improve the quality of their interactions and address challenges in their personal or professional relationships.

How can you help:

- Improve communication in relationships.

- Address trust and jealousy issues.

- Manage family conflicts constructively.

- Develop teamwork skills in work environments.

- Improve emotional connection and intimacy in relationships.

- Facilitate the transition to new stages of life in family relationships.

How does this work:

- Evaluation of Relational Dynamics: An initial evaluation of the dynamics and challenges present in the relationships is carried out, identifying areas of improvement and strengths.

- Development of Relational Objectives: In collaboration with clients, specific objectives are established to improve key aspects of relationships and achieve positive change.

- Improvement of Communication Skills: We work on the development of effective communication skills, active listening and emotional expression.

- Addressing Conflicts and Challenges: Strategies and techniques are provided to address conflicts constructively, identifying solutions and mutual commitments.

- Strengthening Emotional Connection: We work to improve emotional connection and mutual understanding, strengthening emotional ties in relationships.

- Development of Strategies for Change: Concrete action plans are created that involve changes in behavior and habits to improve relational dynamics.

- Continuous Monitoring and Evaluation: The Relationship Coaching process includes continuous monitoring to evaluate progress, adjust strategies as necessary, and provide ongoing support.

Relationship Coaching is a valuable tool for those seeking to improve the quality of their personal relationships, develop effective communication skills, and address interpersonal challenges.

PERSONAL FINANCE COACHING

Personal Finance Coaching is a specialized coaching discipline that focuses on supporting individuals in effectively managing their financial resources, making informed financial decisions and planning to achieve specific financial goals.

What is it for:

Personal Finance Coaching serves to improve financial health, develop solid financial habits, set realistic financial goals, and promote conscious and responsible money management.

Goals:

- Develop healthy financial habits.

- Create and follow a personal budget.

- Save and invest strategically.

- Address debts and improve credit management.

- Plan for short and long term goals.

- Improve understanding of financial concepts.

Who is it intended for:

Personal Finance Coaching is intended for individuals seeking to improve their financial situation, learn to manage their money effectively, and work toward specific financial goals.

How can you help:

- Create and follow a personal budget plan.

- Develop strategies to save and invest intelligently.

- Address impulsive spending habits and improve financial discipline.

- Plan for important financial events, such as purchasing a home or retirement.

- Improve understanding of financial concepts and informed decision making.

How does this work:

- Analysis of the Financial Situation: A detailed evaluation of the current financial situation is carried out, including income, expenses, debts and assets.

- Establishment of Financial Goals: In collaboration with the client, specific financial goals are established in the short, medium and long term.

- Development of a Personal Budget: We work on creating a personal budget that reflects financial goals and allows for effective money management.

- Financial Education: Education is provided on key financial concepts, savings and investment strategies, and tools for financial management.

- Planning for the Future: A comprehensive financial plan is developed that addresses retirement planning, debt management and other relevant aspects.

- Monitoring and Adjustments: The Personal Finance Coaching process includes regular monitoring to evaluate progress, make adjustments to the plan as necessary, and provide ongoing support.

- Promotion of Financial Discipline: We work on the development of financial discipline, resistance to the temptations of unnecessary spending and the adoption of healthy financial habits.

Personal Finance Coaching is a valuable tool for those looking to improve their financial situation, learn to make informed decisions, and work toward a stronger financial future.

DIVERSITY AND INCLUSION COACHING

Diversity and Inclusion Coaching is a specialty of coaching that focuses on supporting individuals, leaders and teams in creating inclusive work environments, managing diversity and promoting equity in the workplace.

What is it for:

Diversity and Inclusion Coaching serves to foster awareness and understanding of diversity, promote equal opportunity, address unconscious bias, and build organizational cultures that celebrate and value diversity.

Goals:

- Promote awareness and understanding of diversity.

- Develop inclusive leadership skills.

- Promote the creation of inclusive organizational cultures.

- Address unconscious biases and barriers to inclusion.

- Improve collaboration and intercultural communication.

- Support equal opportunities in the workplace.

Who is it intended for:

Diversity and Inclusion Coaching is intended for leaders, teams and professionals seeking to improve diversity management in the workplace and create more inclusive work environments.

How can you help:

- Develop training programs on diversity and inclusion.

- Facilitate the understanding of different perspectives and experiences.

- Address conflicts related to diversity and inclusion.

- Promote equity in hiring and promotion processes.

- Improve intercultural communication in work teams.

- Develop strategies to retain and promote diversity in the organization.

How does this work:

- Evaluation of Organizational Culture: An evaluation of the organizational culture is carried out to identify areas for improvement in the management of diversity and inclusion.

- Development of Awareness and Empathy: We work on developing awareness about diversity, addressing prejudices and promoting empathy towards different perspectives and experiences.

- Inclusive Leadership Training: Training is provided

for leaders on inclusive leadership practices, including managing diverse teams and promoting equity.

- Development of Training Programs: Diversity and inclusion training programs are designed and implemented for all staff, addressing key topics and providing practical tools.

- Addressing Conflicts and Challenges: We work on identifying and addressing conflicts related to diversity, promoting constructive resolution and mutual understanding.

- Development of Organizational Strategies: We collaborate with the organization to develop strategies and policies that promote diversity and inclusion at all levels.

- Continuous Monitoring and Evaluation: The Diversity and Inclusion Coaching process includes continuous monitoring to evaluate progress, adjust strategies as necessary and ensure the sustainability of initiatives.

Diversity and Inclusion Coaching is a fundamental tool for organizations seeking to create more inclusive, equitable and respectful work environments for the diversity of their employees.

EMOTIONAL INTELLIGENCE COACHING

Emotional Intelligence Coaching is a specialized coaching discipline that focuses on supporting individuals in the development of emotional and social skills, the effective management of emotions and the improvement of interpersonal relationships.

What is it for:

Emotional Intelligence Coaching serves to strengthen self-awareness, improve emotional management, foster empathy and develop social skills that contribute to personal well-being and success in various areas of life.

Goals:

- Develop emotional self-awareness.

- Improve effective management of emotions.

- Promote empathy and emotional understanding towards others.

- Develop social and interpersonal skills.

- Promote decision making based on emotional intelligence.

- Improve resilience and emotional adaptability.

Who is it intended for:

Emotional Intelligence Coaching is intended for anyone seeking to strengthen their emotional skills, improve their handling of challenging emotional situations, and enhance their interpersonal relationships.

How can you help:

- Develop self-awareness of one's own emotions and reactions.

- Improve stress and anxiety management.

- Promote empathy and emotional understanding towards others.

- Develop effective communication skills.

- Improve conflict resolution and negotiation.

- Enhance self-confidence and self-esteem.

How does this work:

- Evaluation of Emotional Competencies: An initial evaluation of the individual's emotional competencies is carried out, identifying areas of strength and opportunities for improvement.

- Development of Emotional Self-Awareness: We work on the recognition and understanding of one's own emotions, identifying patterns and automatic reactions.

- Effective Emotion Management: Strategies and techniques are provided to effectively manage emotions, including stress management and emotional regulation.

- Development of Empathy and Social Skills: Empathy towards others is encouraged and social skills are developed to improve interpersonal relationships.

- Training in Effective Communication: We work on the development of communication skills that facilitate the clear expression of emotions and mutual understanding.

- Conflict Resolution and Negotiation: Strategies for constructive conflict resolution and the development of negotiation skills based on emotional intelligence are addressed.

- Enhancement of Self-Confidence and Self-Esteem: Aspects related to self-confidence and self-esteem are worked on, promoting a positive self-image.

- Continuous Monitoring and Support: The Emotional Intelligence Coaching process includes continuous monitoring to evaluate progress, adjust strategies as necessary and provide ongoing support.

Emotional Intelligence Coaching is a valuable tool for those seeking to develop emotional skills fundamental to personal well-being and success in various aspects of life.

COACHING IN SUSTAINABLE DEVELOPMENT

Sustainable Development Coaching is a specialized coaching discipline that focuses on supporting individuals, leaders and organizations in the integration of sustainable and responsible practices in their activities, promoting a balance between economic growth, social responsibility and environmental preservation. atmosphere.

What is it for:

Sustainable Development Coaching serves to guide individuals and organizations towards more sustainable practices, promoting ethical decision-making, social responsibility and contribution to environmental well-being.

Goals:

- Integrate sustainable practices into operations and processes.

- Develop strategies for corporate social responsibility.

- Promote ethical and conscious decision-making.

- Promote environmental awareness and the reduction of negative impacts.

- Improve efficiency in the use of resources and waste management.

- Contribute to the well-being of society and the environment.

Who is it intended for:

Sustainable Development Coaching is intended for business leaders, entrepreneurs, professionals and organizations that seek to align their activities with sustainable principles and contribute positively to society and the environmental environment.

How can you help:

- Develop and implement corporate social responsibility strategies.

- Integrate sustainable practices in the supply chain and operations.

- Promote environmental awareness and carbon footprint reduction.

- Improve efficiency in the use of resources and waste management.

- Facilitate the transition towards more sustainable business models.

- Develop and communicate ethical and sustainable values.

How does this work:

- Evaluation of Current Practices: An evaluation of current

practices and policies is carried out to identify areas for improvement in terms of sustainability and social responsibility.

- Development of Sustainable Strategies: In collaboration with the client, sustainable strategies and objectives are designed that align with the values and goals of the organization or individual.

- Integration in Operations and Processes: We work on the practical integration of sustainable measures in operations, processes and daily decision making.

- Cultural Change and Communication: A cultural change towards sustainability is encouraged, effectively communicating sustainable values and the importance of responsible practices.

- Impact Monitoring and Evaluation: Metrics are established to monitor the impact of sustainable initiatives, continually evaluating progress and making adjustments as necessary.

- Development of Sustainable Leadership Skills: We work on the development of leadership skills that encourage ethical decision-making and the promotion of sustainable practices.

- Collaboration with Stakeholders: Collaboration with various interested parties, such as employees, customers, suppliers and the community, is promoted to strengthen the positive impact on sustainability.

- Continuous Monitoring and Continuous Improvement: The Sustainable Development Coaching process includes continuous monitoring to evaluate long-term impact, make adjustments as necessary and encourage continuous improvement.

Sustainable Development Coaching is a valuable tool for those who seek to align their actions and practices with the principles of sustainability, contributing to the well-being of society and the environment.

Entrepreneurship Coaching

Entrepreneurship Coaching is a specialized coaching discipline that focuses on supporting entrepreneurs, businessmen and professionals who seek to develop and grow their business projects.

What is it for:

Entrepreneurship Coaching serves to guide entrepreneurs in the creation and development of their businesses, overcome specific challenges in the business environment, and maximize the potential for success in their business initiatives.

Goals:

- Develop and validate business ideas.

- Develop and execute effective business plans.

- Overcome common challenges of entrepreneurship.

- Enhance leadership and decision-making skills.

- Optimize marketing and sales strategies.

- Achieve sustainable growth of entrepreneurship.

Who is it intended for:

Entrepreneurship Coaching is intended for entrepreneurs, startup founders, small business owners and professionals looking to launch or grow their business projects.

How can you help:

- Develop the business vision and strategy.

- Identify and address specific obstacles to entrepreneurship.

- Define an effective approach to marketing the product or service.

- Optimize time and resource management in the business context.

- Improve negotiation skills and establish strategic partners.

- Promote innovation and adaptability in a changing business environment.

How does this work:

- Analysis and Validation of the Business Idea: The viability and potential of the business idea is evaluated, identifying opportunities and challenges.

- Development of the Business Strategy: We work on defining the vision, mission and business strategy, establishing clear goals and objectives.

- Planning and Execution of the Business Plan: A detailed business plan is prepared, and support is provided in the effective implementation and execution of the plan.

- Business Challenge Management: Specific entrepreneurship challenges are addressed, such as financial management, customer acquisition, and team building.

- Optimization of Marketing and Sales Strategies: Marketing and sales strategies adapted to the market are worked on, including tactics to increase visibility and customer acquisition.

- Development of Business Leadership Skills: Focuses on the development of leadership and effective decision-making skills to direct the growth of the company.

- Innovation and Adaptability: Innovation and adaptability are encouraged in a changing business environment, identifying opportunities for continuous improvement.

- Continuous Monitoring and Adjustments: The Entrepreneurship Coaching process includes continuous monitoring to evaluate progress, make adjustments as necessary, and provide ongoing support.

Entrepreneurship Coaching is a valuable tool for those seeking to become successful entrepreneurs, maximizing the potential of their business initiatives and overcoming the challenges inherent to the world of entrepreneurship.

CREATIVITY COACHING

Creativity Coaching is a specialized coaching discipline that focuses on stimulating and enhancing the creativity of individuals, teams and organizations. It seeks to unlock innovative thinking, overcome creative barriers and encourage a more creative approach to problem solving and decision making.

What is it for:

Creativity Coaching serves to unleash creative potential, develop innovative thinking, overcome creative blocks and foster an environment conducive to the generation of novel ideas.

Goals:

- Develop individual and collective creativity.

- Overcome creative blocks and limitations.

- Promote the generation of innovative ideas.

- Integrate creativity in problem solving.

- Improve the capacity for adaptation and mental flexibility.

- Stimulate a creative work environment.

Who is it intended for:

Creativity Coaching is intended for individuals, teams and organizations that seek to enhance their creative capacity, whether to solve specific problems, promote innovation or improve the quality of the ideas generated.

How can you help:

- Stimulate the generation of original ideas.

- Overcome mental blocks and limiting thought patterns.

- Develop a more creative approach to problem solving.

- Promote collaboration and creative thinking as a team.

- Integrate creativity into decision-making processes.

- Establish a work environment that encourages creativity.

How does this work:

- Exploration of Creative Blocks: Mental blocks and limiting thought patterns that may be hindering creativity are identified.

- Stimulation of the Imagination: Techniques are used to stimulate the imagination and open new perspectives, encouraging the generation of original ideas.

- Development of Creative Skills: Specific skills related to creativity are worked on, such as observation, association of ideas, and mental flexibility.

- Integration of Creativity in Decision Making: Strategies are provided to incorporate creativity in decision-making processes, contributing to more innovative solutions.

- Promotion of Creative Collaboration: Collaboration between individuals and teams is promoted, creating an environment where ideas can flow freely and be improved jointly.

- Practical Application in Projects: We work on the practical application of creativity in specific projects, integrating creative approaches in solving problems and generating solutions.

- Evaluation and Feedback: The Creativity Coaching process includes continuous evaluation and feedback to adjust strategies, overcome challenges and improve creative capacity over time.

- Creative Organizational Culture: We work on developing an organizational culture that encourages and celebrates creativity, recognizing the importance of innovation at all levels.

Creativity Coaching is a valuable tool for those seeking to enhance their creative capacity and adopt a more innovative approach in their personal and professional lives.

Coaching in Change Management

Change Management Coaching is a specialized coaching discipline that focuses on supporting individuals, teams and organizations in the effective management of change processes. It seeks to facilitate adaptation, overcome resistance and maximize success in moments of organizational transformation.

What is it for:

Change Management Coaching serves to guide individuals and teams through change processes, promoting acceptance, adaptability and effective leadership during organizational transitions.

Goals:

- Facilitate adaptation and acceptance of change.

- Minimize resistance and fear associated with change.

- Develop leadership skills during change processes.

- Maximize effectiveness in the implementation of organizational changes.

- Improve communication and management of expectations during transitions.

Who is it intended for:

Change Management Coaching is intended for leaders, teams and professionals who face organizational change processes, mergers, restructuring or other transformations that impact the work environment.

How can you help:

- Develop strategies to effectively communicate the change.

- Minimize resistance and fear associated with change.

- Facilitate the adaptation and acceptance of new processes.

- Develop leadership skills in times of change.

- Improve expectations management and internal communication.

- Maximize effectiveness in the implementation of organizational changes.

How does this work:

- Analysis of the Change Situation: The nature and scope of the change is evaluated, identifying areas of impact and possible resistance.

- Development of Communication Strategies: Effective communication strategies are worked on to inform and educate those involved about the change, addressing concerns and maintaining transparency.

- Resistance Management: Specific resistances and concerns are addressed, identifying solutions and strategies to mitigate resistance to change.

- Leadership Development during Change: We work on developing the leadership skills necessary to guide teams through change, including managing emotions and inspiring trust.

- Individual and Team Support: Individual and team support is provided to manage the emotions associated with change, offering a space for expression and development of coping strategies.

- Development of Adaptability Skills: Adaptability and mental flexibility skills are worked on, helping individuals and teams to positively adjust to new realities.

- Continuous Evaluation and Adjustments: The Change Management Coaching process includes continuous evaluation to adjust strategies as necessary, addressing changing dynamics and ensuring successful implementation.

- Culture of Learning and Continuous Improvement: A culture of learning and continuous improvement is encouraged, where change processes are seen as opportunities for growth and innovation.

Change Management Coaching is an essential tool for those seeking to lead and adapt effectively during organizational change processes, contributing to success and stability in constantly evolving environments.

CONFLICT RESOLUTION COACHING

Conflict Resolution Coaching is a specialized coaching discipline that focuses on supporting individuals, teams and leaders in the effective management of interpersonal and organizational conflicts. It seeks to develop communication skills, promote mutual understanding and find constructive solutions to conflicting challenges.

What is it for:

Conflict Resolution Coaching serves to improve the ability to manage and resolve conflicts constructively, promoting a positive work environment, healthy relationships and effective collaboration.

Goals:

- Develop effective communication skills.

- Promote mutual understanding between parties in conflict.

- Identify and address the underlying causes of conflicts.

- Facilitate the search for constructive and mutually beneficial solutions.

- Improve emotional management during conflict situations.

- Establish a positive and collaborative work environment.

Who is it intended for:

Conflict Resolution Coaching is intended for individuals, teams and leaders who face challenges related to interpersonal conflicts, whether in the workplace or in any other context.

How can you help:

- Improve the ability to express ideas and opinions clearly.

- Develop empathy and understanding towards the perspectives of others.

- Identify behavior patterns that contribute to conflicts.

- Facilitate open and constructive communication between parties in conflict.

- Promote the search for collaborative solutions instead of opposing positions.

- Establish practices and standards to prevent recurring conflicts.

How does this work:

- Evaluation of the Conflict Situation: The nature and context of the conflict is analyzed, identifying the parties involved, their perspectives and the underlying causes.

- Development of Communication Skills: We work on the development of effective communication skills, including active listening, the clear expression of ideas and the management of emotions during communication.

- Analysis of Underlying Causes: The underlying causes of the conflict are identified, exploring patterns of behavior and beliefs that may contribute to the conflict dynamics.

- Facilitation of Mutual Understanding: It seeks to foster mutual understanding between parties in conflict, promoting the recognition of different perspectives and empathy towards the experiences of others.

- Development of Resolution Strategies: Specific strategies for conflict resolution are explored and developed, including collaborative approaches, the search for solutions and the effective management of disagreements.

- Practical Application in Real Situations: We work on the practical application of conflict resolution strategies in real situations, providing guidance and support during the process.

- Establishment of Preventive Standards and Practices: We collaborate in the establishment of standards and practices that prevent future conflicts, promoting a positive and collaborative work environment.

- Continuous Monitoring and Evaluation: The Conflict Resolution Coaching process includes continuous monitoring to evaluate progress, make adjustments as necessary and ensure long-term effectiveness.

Conflict Resolution Coaching is a valuable tool for those seeking to transform conflict situations into opportunities for learning and growth, promoting healthy relationships and a positive work environment.

TRANSFORMATION COACHING

Transformation Coaching is a specialized coaching discipline that focuses on supporting individuals, teams and organizations in processes of deep and sustainable change. It seeks to facilitate personal and organizational transformation, promoting development, innovation and adaptation to new realities.

What is it for:

Transformation Coaching serves to guide individuals and organizations through significant change processes, fostering personal growth, adaptability and the creation of a desired future.

Goals:

- Facilitate personal and organizational transformation.

- Develop a clear vision of the desired future.

- Promote transformational leadership.

- Promote continuous learning and innovation.

- Improve resilience and adaptability to change.

- Build an organizational culture oriented to

transformation.

Who is it intended for:

Transformation Coaching is intended for leaders, teams and individuals seeking to make significant changes in their personal life or in the organizational context.

How can you help:

- Develop a clear vision of the future and transformative goals.

- Overcome resistance to change and encourage acceptance.

- Develop transformational leadership skills.

- Promote creativity and innovation in problem solving.

- Improve the ability to adapt to new realities.

- Build an organizational culture based on transformation.

How does this work:

- Clarification of Vision and Goals: We work on defining a clear vision of the desired future, identifying transformative goals that guide the change process.

- Exploration and Overcoming Resistance: Resistance and fears associated with change are addressed, exploring limiting beliefs and developing strategies to overcome obstacles.

- Development of Transformational Leadership Skills: We work on the development of leadership skills that foster inspiration, shared vision and mobilization towards transformative goals.

- Promotion of Creativity and Innovation: An environment that promotes creativity and innovation is fostered, stimulating original thinking and the search for unconventional solutions.

- Adaptability and Resilience to Change: Skills are developed to adapt to new realities, improving emotional resilience and the ability to manage uncertainty.

- Change of Beliefs and Paradigms: We work on changing beliefs and paradigms that may limit the transformation process, promoting an open and receptive mentality to change.

- Accompaniment in the Change Process: Continuous support is provided throughout the change process, offering tools, resources and guidance to face challenges and celebrate achievements.

- Development of a Transformative Organizational Culture: At the organizational level, work is being done to build a culture that values continuous transformation, encourages collaboration and stimulates innovation.

- Continuous Monitoring and Evaluation: Transformation Coaching includes continuous monitoring to evaluate progress, make adjustments as necessary and ensure the sustainability of the transformation.

Transformation Coaching is a powerful tool for those seeking to make significant changes in their lives or organizational environment, promoting continuous development and the creation of a future more aligned with their aspirations and values.

COACHING AND MINDFULNESS

Mindfulness Coaching is a specialized coaching discipline that integrates mindfulness principles and practices to promote full attention, awareness, and effective stress management. This approach helps individuals and teams cultivate mindful presence in their personal and professional lives.

What is it for:

Mindfulness Coaching serves to develop mindfulness skills, improve stress management, foster mental clarity and promote greater well-being in everyday life.

Goals:

- Cultivate full attention and awareness in the present moment.

- Improve stress and anxiety management.

- Develop emotional self-regulation skills.

- Promote mental clarity and conscious decision making.

- Improve quality of life and general well-being.

Who is it intended for:

Mindfulness Coaching is intended for anyone who wants to incorporate mindfulness practices into their daily life, whether to improve their emotional well-being, manage stress or enhance their performance at work.

How can you help:

- Develop the ability to be present in the current moment.

- Improve stress and anxiety management.

- Cultivate attention and concentration.

- Promote emotional self-regulation.

- Improve the quality of interpersonal relationships.

- Support work performance and conscious decision making.

How does this work:

- Mindfulness Practices: Mindfulness techniques are introduced and practiced, which may include mindfulness meditation, conscious breathing, and other practices aimed at cultivating conscious presence.

- Exploration of Mental Patterns: We work on the identification of automatic mental patterns, recurring thoughts and habitual reactions, promoting self-awareness.

- Stress and Anxiety Management: Mindfulness strategies are provided to manage stress and anxiety, including conscious response to challenging situations.

- Cultivation of Attention and Concentration: Techniques are developed to improve attention and concentration, allowing individuals to focus more effectively on specific tasks.

- Development of Emotional Self-Regulation: We work on cultivating emotional awareness and the ability to consciously respond to emotions, instead of reacting automatically.

- Application in the Work and Personal Environment: Ways to integrate mindfulness practices in the work and personal environment are explored, adapting them to individual and professional needs.

- Improvement of Interpersonal Relationships: The application of mindfulness is encouraged to improve interpersonal relationships, promoting empathy, active listening and conscious communication.

- Continuous Monitoring and Reinforcement: The Mindfulness Coaching process includes continuous monitoring to evaluate the integration of mindfulness practices into daily life and make adjustments as necessary.

Mindfulness Coaching offers valuable tools for those seeking to cultivate mindfulness, improve stress management, and promote greater well-being in their personal and professional lives.

Coaching in Interpersonal Communication

Interpersonal Communication Coaching is a specialized coaching discipline that focuses on improving the communication skills of individuals and teams. It seeks to strengthen the ability to express oneself effectively, listen with empathy and build positive interpersonal relationships.

What is it for:

Interpersonal Communication Coaching serves to develop effective communication skills, improve the quality of interpersonal relationships, and encourage clear and empathetic communication.

Goals:

- Develop clear and effective expression skills.

- Promote active listening and empathy.

- Improve the ability to manage conflicts constructively.

- Build positive interpersonal relationships.

- Optimize communication in professional and personal environments.

Who is it intended for:

Interpersonal Communication Coaching is intended for individuals, leaders, teams and professionals who seek to improve their communication skills in various contexts, whether in the workplace or in personal relationships.

How can you help:

- Develop skills to express ideas clearly and persuasively.

- Encourage active listening and understanding of others' perspectives.

- Improve the ability to manage disagreements and conflicts constructively.

- Optimize non-verbal communication to transmit effective messages.

- Build relationships of trust based on open and transparent communication.

- Adapt the communication style to different audiences and contexts.

How does this work:

- Communication Style Analysis: Individual communication styles are evaluated, identifying strengths and areas for improvement in expression and listening.

- Development of Expression Skills: We work on developing skills to express ideas and messages in a clear, persuasive way and adapted to the context.

- Promotion of Active Listening and Empathy: Active listening practices are promoted, encouraging empathy and understanding of the perspectives of others.

- Constructive Conflict Management: Strategies and tools

are provided to manage disagreements and conflicts constructively, seeking collaborative solutions.

- Optimization of Non-Verbal Communication: We work on improving non-verbal communication, including gestures, facial expressions and posture, to reinforce the message transmitted.

- Adaptation to Different Audiences: The ability to adapt the communication style to different audiences and contexts is developed, considering the needs and preferences of the recipients.

- Building Trusted Relationships: Focuses on building interpersonal relationships based on trust, transparency and open communication.

- Communication Practices in Real Situations: Communication skills are applied and practiced in real situations, receiving feedback and adjusting accordingly.

- Continuous Monitoring and Improvement: The Interpersonal Communication Coaching process includes continuous monitoring to evaluate progress, make adjustments as necessary and encourage continuous improvement.

Interpersonal Communication Coaching is a valuable tool for those who seek to strengthen their communication skills, improve the quality of their relationships and be more effective in transmitting and receiving messages in different environments.

PARENTING COACHING

Parenting Coaching is a specialized discipline of coaching that focuses on supporting parents and caregivers in developing parenting skills, managing family challenges and building positive relationships with their children.

What is it for:

Parenting Coaching helps parents and caregivers improve their parenting skills, address specific parenting challenges, and foster a healthy family environment.

Goals:

- Develop effective parenting skills.

- Improve communication with children.

- Address specific parenting challenges.

- Encourage the building of positive relationships.

- Promote a harmonious and supportive family environment.

Who is it intended for:

Parenting Coaching is intended for parents, caregivers

and families seeking guidance and support in raising their children, whether in conflict resolution, behavior management or improving family communication.

How can you help:

- Develop skills to set effective limits.

- Improve communication and understanding with children.

- Address specific parenting challenges, such as behavior management.

- Promote the construction of self-esteem and social skills in children.

- Establish effective family routines and structures.

- Manage the transition to new stages of children's development.

How does this work:

- Parenting Skills Assessment: An assessment of current parenting skills is performed, identifying areas of strength and those that could benefit from development.

- Development of Communication Strategies: Strategies are worked on to improve communication with children, including active listening and the effective expression of expectations and feelings.

- Establishment of Limits and Norms: Helps in establishing clear limits and norms, providing strategies for managing behavior and promoting responsibility.

- Addressing Specific Parenting Challenges: Specific challenges that may arise in parenting are addressed, such as sleep problems, sibling conflicts, or screen time management.

- Promotion of Positive Relationships: We work on building positive relationships with children, promoting empathy, emotional support and building self-esteem.

- Management of Transitions and Changes: Support is provided during important transitions, such as changes in family dynamics, moves or stages of children's development.

- Development of Self-Care Skills: Focuses on the development of self-care skills for parents, recognizing the importance of their well-being in effective parenting.

- Creation of Family Routines and Structures: We collaborate in the creation of effective family routines and structures, providing stability and predictability in daily life.

- Ongoing Monitoring and Adjustments: The Parenting Coaching process includes continuous monitoring to evaluate progress, make adjustments as necessary, and offer ongoing support as the family evolves.

Parenting Coaching offers a space of support and guidance for parents, helping them face challenges, improve their parenting skills and foster a healthy and harmonious family environment.

NAVIGATING
THE COACHING
UNIVERSE

And that's it for our journey through some of the most important and interesting aspects of coaching. In the fascinating journey we have taken throughout this book, we have explored the vast and enriching universe of coaching. From its general foundations to specialized disciplines ranging from parenting to mindfulness, we have unraveled the infinite possibilities this transformative practice offers.

The Power of Coaching:

At its core, coaching is a catalyst for positive change. It is a collaborative alliance between coach and client, aimed at unlocking potential, overcoming obstacles and achieving goals. More than just a tool, coaching is a life philosophy that drives personal growth, self-reflection and continuous improvement.

Twenty Disciplines, One Objective:

We have explored twenty different disciplines of coaching,

each designed to address specific aspects of our lives. From Life Coaching, which invites us to chart a meaningful path, to Parenting Coaching, which guides us in the art of raising children, each discipline offers a unique and valuable approach.

Executive Coaching stands as a beacon in business leadership, while Interpersonal Communication Coaching weaves stronger ties into the fabric of human relationships. Health and Wellness Coaching reminds us of the importance of taking care of ourselves, while Transformation Coaching awakens the flame of personal evolution.

The Magic of Continuous Exploration:

Coaching is not limited to a single path; It is a vast landscape full of paths to discover. In each discipline, we find valuable tools, effective strategies and, above all, a constant reminder that change is possible and growth is inevitable.

The Invitation to Adventure:

As we conclude this journey, the invitation to delve deeper into the wonderful world of coaching resonates strongly. Each page we have explored has been a step on this journey, but the real discovery is in continuing beyond these words.

I encourage you not to see the end of this book as a point of arrival, but as the beginning of a new phase in your own quest for development and fulfillment. Coaching is a beacon that will guide you through the uncharted waters of your life, offering support, clarity and direction every step of the way.

Discover Your Own Path:

Coaching is not a one-size-fits-all formula; It is a toolbox that allows you to design your own path. Dare to explore, to question, to grow. Find the discipline that resonates with you, but don't limit yourself. The beauty of coaching lies in its adaptability to your unique needs and aspirations.

A Future of Infinite Possibilities:

The coaching universe is full of infinite possibilities. Imagine a future where your goals are achieved, your challenges overcome and your life transformed. This is the gift that coaching has to offer: a constant journey of discovery that takes you beyond your self-imposed limits.

Enter the Wonderful World of Coaching:

So I invite you to dive deeper into this wonderful world of coaching. Discover more disciplines, explore new territories and embrace the opportunity to continually grow. The magic is in the journey, and coaching is the compass that will guide you through it.

Always remember that the journey never ends; Every day is a new opportunity to learn, grow and become the best version of yourself. Let this conclusion be the beginning of your own story of transformation through coaching. Go forth, intrepid explorers of human potential!